8

LAWS OF CORPORATE AMERICA

The laws to moving through complicated
situations and coming out on top.

ROBERT GREENE

Thank You!

Thanks For Reading

Hello, this message is from Robert Greene. I hope that you enjoy this Book. It is my intention to provide information that my readers will enjoy and benefit from.

I am thankfull when people read my books and I love it when my readers leave a review. Please feel free leave a review after reading. This allows me know what you liked about my book so I can work on constantly improving.

What is Corporate America?

Do you remember when you had your first thought of Corporate America and working there? A job of high importance came to mind, maybe even wearing a suit and working in a fancy office. We can build up these ideas that can be as close to the truth as what we see on TV or as far as the next state over. The sad truth in the matter of this place is, although it has its perks and benefits, it has about as much politics and cliques as the high school cafeteria.

When thinking about life after high school we always imagined that the real world wouldn't have as many barriers allowing us to enjoy the experience. The cool kids, although they were completely outnumbered by the kids that weren't, had the approval of the staff to lead and make decisions for the overall student body. You might remember being frustrated by this because these students weren't as bright or as knowledgeable as you or your peers about what they were running or leading. The staff's only job was to teach and ignore the many obstacles in place put by the people they put there to speak and lead the group or teams. One might laugh at the comparison of Corporate America to high school, but to many that have lived it, they know it's a spot-on truth when comparing to the politics. There are many situations and day-to-day processes that either work against you or allow you to make it to the next class project.

Why do you want
to be apart of it?

Why wouldn't you want to be a part of Corporate America? When people have a corporate job they are the first ones to speak about their place of employment when talking with friends and families. They wear it like a badge of honor as though people all want know of their courageous battle stories that take place day to day. Some are already waiting to answer the next question: "What's it like to work there?" Then prepare yourself next for 15 minutes as this person rambles about all of the above, putting the truth in a nice box with a lovely bow on the top. The other reason a person might want to work for Corporate America is because of the benefits and pay. Who wants to work for a place that has no job security or benefits to help position your family better?

The greatest feeling is when you get a call-back for a position. The next step will be what to wear and say to make these people of importance feel you are important enough to be hired. Most of us who have had these kinds of jobs know that the great feelings of accomplishment become slim to none later. We hear of the harsh stories and rumors but still somehow want to be a part of the bigger picture. The incredible break-through happens and you get hired. With this you get a salary and benefits. You know now that you will have a set amount of steady income each month and your benefits will be available after 90 days. Your first day normally involves them parading you around the office to meet people who will either work against or become an alliance. The paperwork is filed and you're now working in Corporate America. Most of your conversations at dinner when asked about the new gig will end with saying that everyone is cool and things are good. Weeks go by now and you have started to get the hang of things and have pinpointed the people in the office and their roles. You search for patterns to put in place to ease the anxiety when a grey area presents itself. All of the woodwork is showing and the walls are talking; you hear people who are happy and those who believe they have the solutions. The ones who like you feel the need to inform you of people and things to watch out for. The people to watch out for watch you to see where you fall in their company. Your list of things to get done never get done because one thing is coming in as the other one is going. The meetings that happen about getting things done never get done. The year moves forward. This next step is not to tell you things you already don't know for those who live it, but maybe to give you an insight into what's happening and how to survive if you're new. They are called the 8 Laws of Corporate America.

LAW 1

Avoid the crabs (Keeping the two-faced and keep the grass short)

We have all heard of the saying crabs in a bucket, and if you aren't familiar with this logic it's quite simple. When you reach into a bucket to pull out the crab you want, there will always be other crabs latching on to hold the crab you want. Sometimes the grip from the other crabs can be so great that the crab you want loses parts when you try to separate them. The metaphor isn't a pretty vision but neither is it when applied to your work environment. You will have many people who are around you who are just there to keep an eye on what you are doing to make sure you don't get any credit without them taking part as well. Another name that comes to mind when describing these people is called two-faced. For many of you who might be new to the term, this is when a person comes as a friend of yours. The minute you are not around they will bash you and belittle your efforts. These people will even take credit for your work if they were seen working minor parts, thus giving the appearance of

14

having two faces. One face they greet you with and another they show others. One might ask how to deal with people like this. The answer is: you don't. They are their own living, walking, breathing hazard sign. Little do they know the same people they bash all communicate and are aware of their childish behavior. Your job is not to make efforts of changing this person or people; it's not what you get paid for. Learn to ignore them, but don't lose track of them when you share a space. Keep your grass short so you can see the snakes as well.

LAW
2

Know your battles
(Don't argue with idiots)

When you first find out that someone might be spreading a fictitious rumor or attempting to throw you under a bus, your first reaction is to confront the person. The rude awakening of a two-faced person in your circle is never a good feeling. Some of these people should get Oscars for the efforts they put into scrambling radars. It's a sad thought that people like this actually can have a successful career. "The upper management would never let people like this exist knowing of their actions," you're thinking. Another truth be told, many of your managers know exactly who they were hiring and they call it stirring up the pot. So why don't I confront them if it's all a lie? The reason you don't confront this person is because now the person knows what you know. Let's say you're playing a game of cards and you by chance put out the wrong card or cards. Do you think you just helped yourself or made your winning very difficult? In some games people will even say, "I know you have a king," demanding their victory. In most cases, if a crab knows you caught wind of their actions they will want some kind of response from you. When I say do and say nothing, I mean just that; no dagger eyes, either. Battles come in many forms and the key is for you to recognize what kind it is. Some battles are right in plain eyesight. What's hard about avoiding an obvious fight in the corner office? Giving that person a piece of my mind, your mother might say. The other kind might be internal and a mental battlefield. The mental kinds are the worst types. These types of battles have upper management written all over them. They can be the focus of most meetings, and if the meeting's about you they will devise a plan to either promote or demote/fire you. When a crab looks at you they look first to see if there is any importance you can serve them, not the team. Does this person have what it takes to be a crab? You being a good person and hard worker is not their focus. If having a good career were built on good morals

18

and character, our government wouldn't need our vote. Trust me, you will know right away where you fall in their world. Don't lie to yourself; their actions will speak louder than yours. Your bosses and them meeting a lot might bring you stress and make you wonder what's going to happen next. Simply said, these types of bosses suck and there is no need explaining that over dinner to your family.

"Why is my boss this way?" you might question. This kind of boss derives from when a two-faced person or crab reaches a high position. Don't kill yourself trying to prove yourself to these idiots. Remember, most crabs hire other crabs and they know who's not one. First off, having any boss over you is always a hard situation. They are the beginning and the end of your worries when you get up in the morning. The sad part is most of us are the kings and queens of our own dominion walking around our homes. The closer we get to the office, driving in traffic, the less power we have and the more insecurities we develop. Remember when you were a kid and you were living under your parents' rules? When you didn't follow them there were always consequences. Your parents might even have said, "Well, one day you will have a career and this is all to prepare you." As much as we love our parents, they could never put this or recreate this headache in the comforts of our homes. Don't live in a nutshell but spot the other crabs fast, and if your boss is a crab then get with the program or get moving. Ever said at home that you are surrounded by idiots at work? Well don't attempt to battle your boss because, if he is a crab, you will lose every time. They aren't worth your time and if they are an idiot then a bigger idiot hired them. Make sense, keep moving like the wind. We all have had jobs we loved but the people made it difficult. The difficult part is leaving bonds and relationships you might have formed at your current em-

20

ployer. Give the feeling a couple of months then see what your leaving sparked, see how many people follow your footsteps. The next job you get, what a relief if the guy or woman hiring you isn't a former crab. They can actually put the team as a higher priority. Ever want to spot if your boss was a former crab in your next meeting or when they are hiring you? See how much they talk. A key trait to observe when spotting a crab is, while in conversation with one, their only focus is to make the conversation about them. You have better things to do with your time than deal with Napoleons and middle child complexes.

LAW 3

Hide your emotions (The loudest ones in the room are the weakest ones in the room)

Disrespect is the hardest thing to ignore when it happens in the working environment. Most of us would rather knock the person's block off the second it happens. When dealing with corporate jobs, they demand a lot of professionalism of everybody. The environments and politics of how things are handled are anything but professional. The term "thrown under the bus" is a situation where it's an expected excuse for some allowing others to wrongfully take the fall when something goes wrong. Bottling your emotions when your name falls in the line-up of many to wait for this bus to trample your week brings many stressful days and nights. One might ask, "Why is it important for me to bottle what I know is right?" The answer to this is simple. What is right, who really is to blame or what really happened might not be what those in charge want to hear, especially if it's them. A lot of times the people above look for what could be a solution or who could take the fall and why we figure out a better solution. We are talking about a place that, most days, has meetings to talk about having more meetings and why we are losing money as a company. You getting wound into a knot and talking to everyone spreading the truth in the matter only sets you apart, showing that you're not a game player. To help you get a better understanding to this childish behavior of this environment, let's go back in time. Remember when you were a kid and your parents were gone, then suddenly something gets broken? Everyone who is home runs into the room to see what happened. The oldest sibling immediately starts to panic because they know that they were the one left in charge. They start to come up with a plan, a lie to cover up the truth, knowing it would only lead to hard penalties when the parents got home. The reality in the situation is apparent: they weren't watching the house or doing their job or being responsible for those who weren't. You telling the truth will only put you in a hole by saying loudly,

"I am a snitch and I am not loyal to the rest of the troop." The time on the plank has come and the parents' car arrives home. Everyone is in a line and now you have two disappointed parents in the room. They have heard everyone's side of the story and what happened. Just to make sure they have everything, the parents ask the same questions another way, seeing if there are any changes in the ending results. The last attempt at the truth, if it matters, they ask the youngest. Why would someone ask the youngest the truth? Well, I think we all know why they would ask the youngest the truth. The loudest ones in the room are always the weakest ones in the room. If anyone is going to fold under pressure and tell the truth it's them because they aren't corrupt by even the politics of a family yet. This also tells you that in an office building, if the CEO wanted to know what really happened they could easy find the truth the same way. Find the loudest one and find the truth. There are two things to guarantee: whoever talks will be eating lunch by themselves and looking for a new job comes the next month.

So let's say you point out everything that is broken and why it is … do you really think you're the only person who sees this roof leaking and printer jamming? The girl napping in her office, the boss enforcing lateness when he is late every day and leaving early? Minding your own business is a saying that goes back to the days of the Bible. According to the King James Bible it states: "And that ye study to be quiet, and to do your own business, and to work with your own hands, as we commanded you;"

Another thing to think about is, let's say you tell the truth every time you are asked as a kid by your parents. Even despite the oldest getting in trouble, they are still left in charge the next time they leave. You just put yourself in a world of hurt and they never forget they, like your boss, get good at making you think they forgot. Don't be surprised when your review comes and it's not what you were expecting or your efforts are not reflected. Don't expect others to stand next to you when you're losing your battle either. When you were a kid did someone come offer to take some of those shoulder punches when the eldest was mad that they sit now in a spotless room missing of all games, cell phone, and other electronics? Despite you doing a noble thing telling the truth in someone's world, things just got worse.

In Corporate America, the same people who might agree with you during your lunch rants are the same people who will be silent after you're replaced. They know that if they speak as loudly as you did they will share your vacation. The people in charge take pride in this kind of treatment and it's call cleaning house. The minute you are let go, the people who you have called friends and family for years will have little to no contact with you out of fear that they aren't showing loyalty to those in charge. Don't take it personal; fear is one of those things many people let control every aspect of their life. What power to have to control whether someone can feed their family or put gas in their car. The reality of this is, yes, they might have the upper hand as long as you are employed with them. Their powers are only limited to the office walls and the minute you enter them. You will find employment somewhere else and you will take care of your family. If you like to keep your job know when to keep your mouth shut or shut up.

28

LAW
4

Build alliances
(Alliances on your level
know about as
much as you)

An alliance is as simple as the saying "having friends in high places." Being the most popular kid in kindergarten might get you a couple more invites to birthday parties. Freshmen year of high school, popularity with the older kids gets you an invite into an exclusive world many don't see. Have your usual day-to-day relationships with others considered to be climbing the ladder as you are. Always be prepared to move into other circles or conversations with those higher up than you. "Well, they don't do the same thing for the company as I do," you might say and that's even better. They are high up and in another area so you might find out exclusive details others wait to hear about come the new quarter or year. Your job is not to mislead people or come across as a user but keep in mind that Corporate America is nothing short of a game. Some play fair and some could not care less about the rules. They make moves and sometimes two if you're not paying attention. Winning isn't always by the book and it sometimes can be because the referee didn't see it. The game of chess comes to mind when building alliances and you're the most important piece on the board. Before you move forward, make sure that all the pieces you move have a reason for being where they are. Don't ever put yourself in harm's way or you will be taken. As many pieces as you move, seeing what the opponent is thinking is only apparent until they do move. Notice how good players play their queen and how it always has a powerful piece guarding it. This piece can stop all attacks from any angle. They are the last retreat for you to move to safety. We have yet to see a queen being guarded by a pawn, the weakest piece, and if it is there's obviously a motive of the picture you don't see yet. Your alliances have to be that powerful piece; they sit in meetings and you don't and they have access and you don't. Keep all information to yourself, as telling another only puts the alliance you're building at risk. The best places to build alliances with these people are usually at their desk and lunch. In the morning most of these people can't live without coffee and you will generally find them here as well, in the kitchen getting their morning fix. Learn to work and pay attention without paying attention to everything. People who have more responsibility in the company either come in really early or stay extremely late, so pick you your avenue.

LAW
5

Build a trust (Who can you trust and paint the roses red)

When dealing with big companies trust is a game of numbers. Not everyone you eat with will hunt with you. In other words, not everyone who was in the music video was with you in the studio writing. You can't expect to trust everyone you encounter, and just because someone invites you to lunch doesn't mean they will pay for it. Sometimes it's just a simple enjoyment of another person's company. Lunch is a good starting point and it lets you get away from people you don't trust, like crabs. Crabs are the last ones you want to know what you really feel. All information to them, good or bad, can serve in their plots to look better.

So let's say you have company of 50 and everyone seems to like everyone. Now, not everyone you eat lunch with you can trust, but they are the place to start when weeding out the process. When we speak of trust we are simply saying trusting with your true feelings of the workplace or a little bit more information about

34

personal situations. To be sure that you're not putting yourself out on a limb, always plant the seed if it's something you're curious about but don't run full into the conversation. If someone bites on the topic and shares their own experience, this means they are willing to trust you as well. When you run into a conversation not allowing the seed to sit, you could be trusting the situation before they trust you.

It's likely to none that you will get your foot out of your mouth if they're loyal to the person you bring up or for the situation you are against. Those who trust you most of the time will say, "Don't ever repeat this," mindful of knowing it could get them in trouble. You then say, "Of course not," and then the conversation of trust happens. Next thing you know you have a trusted buddy. You both share many of the same thoughts and feelings about this awesome place we call work.

Have you ever seen the movie Alice in Wonderland? Well, if you have, then the part where they're painting the roses red should stand out clearly in your mind. Here is where the wrong color of rose bushes were planted and the mistake is noticed, but instead of replanting them the queen's men's plan was set to paint them red. This trust and relationships become part of the paint on the corporate rose bushes. When you go to lunch, the first part of lunch will be spent talking about some roses that you've painted. Meaning it's obvious a problem happened and you had to paint it. They will share with you how they painted quite a bit last week before the CEO noticed. Unlike the queen in the story, most CEOs know the roses are painted red, as they bought the paint. They only get upset when they have noticed you didn't and are happily painting still. When you are hired for a job in Corporate they are looking for rose painters, not problem solvers. The same problems you face when you come will be there when you leave. Employees who complain while painting or forget they were hired to paint … it's off with their heads. Learn to paint and build trust at the same time and it helps the days go faster. Don't lie to yourself; no one likes to paint the bushes but it keeps the CEOs happy and your boss off your back.

37

LAW

6

Keep your life yours
(Not everyone needs to
know your personal life)

This is pretty simple: keep your business to yourself. Its okay to share a little more than usual with those trusted lunch buddies but not with the ones who hired you. Remember, their only concern is that you keep painting roses and going with the grain. "They asked me how my arm was after I slipped on ice last week, so they truly care about me." The exact opposite, actually, and they only wonder if they have to watch over the roses/work you're doing to make sure you're doing theirs correct.

The best answer to this is to keep your answers short and sweet when asked what happened and give minor details only. Huge details only make people digest more. If you tell them of all the doctor visits you might have, well, you just landed yourself on the injured list in their mind. They might even see you as a liability, being annoyed that now they have to work harder or work at all. You're having troubles with your teenage kids or marriage at home. If it's not your trustee at lunch, keep it out of the office. There is a time and a place for personal talk. Allowing your family to fall into the day-to-day small office small talk is not seen as being a professional. Being a professional is being as good as you can with hiding who you really are. Being a professional is doing the opposite of what you really feel every day in the office. Who really wants to act excited to see the same people talk about the same stories and situations for the next two to three years?

Keep this in mind also: if I were a crab looking for anything negative to say about you, you helping me couldn't have been a better solution. People only know about you what you tell them so if you're going to tell people something make sure it's positive. It's hard for a crab to cast darkness on something shining or bright. You being bright is the number one reason

40

crabs latch on to you or sit close enough to grab when the time is near. Crabs only talk about people who are important that's why they choose either themselves or ones they despise. Jealousy is simply love and hate at the same time.

LAW
7

Learn to laugh in the storm (How many recipes do you have for lemon?)

A corporate job is very stressful and Mondays always dictate the course of the week. This is usually the day that your bosses tell you what you didn't or forgot to accomplish the previous week. The weeks that you and your trustees go unharmed are considered the best. Let's say that one month you can feel the fire burning under your butt each day and everything that can go wrong has happened.

If you can't stand the heat in the kitchen then leave is a saying that comes to mind. When you look up from your desk to daydream about the sunny sky with palm trees, all you can see is thunderclouds. The palm trees turn to lemons and it feels like every time a thundercloud strikes lightning, more lemons roll up, surrounding your feet. The lemons can be the day-to-day problems and the thunder is every time something breaks or a bus comes down your street, missing you within inches. The best advice to anyone is to learn to laugh in the middle of the storm and see how many recipes you can make from those lemons. Standing still so you don't get struck by lightning only guarantees you to get struck by lightning. Keep moving, keep working, and if you can find humor in something, laugh at it. The other employees around you admire when those around them can smile when it's not a smiling situation. On a team these people are called the optimistic thinkers. They are the ones who can see a victory when you're down twenty points in the second half of the game. When a huge problem arises you treat it like the big elephant you have to eat. One bite at a time will get you through the entire elephant. The sooner you start today the less you have to eat tomorrow.

44

LAW

8

Don't go against the grain (Only built for the chosen few)

Going against the grain is the most dangerous law of all of them and that's why this one is last. This is the last piece of advice when surviving Corporate America. This is a for sure way to get canned or, as they politically correctly say, "let you go." This is when you speak your mind when you shouldn't and you ignore many of the laws discussed in the previous chapters. A quick way to tell if you are going against the grain is how many people who used to stand next you aren't and how many meetings are you getting about your performance. Whether you are plain sick of painting roses or your boss placing expectations on you he or she doesn't follow, it's always an uncomfortable situation to be in.

When you are going against the grain this is you as a kid telling the truth to your parents, knowing it will bring down the hierarchy. Speaking your mind to whomever before knowing that they have as much to lose and

46

telling you what they feel as well. Not bottling your emotions and telling your boss how painting his rose bushes for him bothers you. In his mind he's wondering well who's going to paint them? Me. The CEO can't see the real color and if he does, it will be off with my head and yours. In most cases whenever you go against the grain it has an immediate consequence. If you're married, go home and tell your wife what you truly feel about shoe shopping with her or the color she chose for the bathroom. Have fun lying on your victory couch with the pillow you didn't want and cat you didn't buy. Tell your husband no Sunday football or the new time limits on the man cave when the kids are home. Have fun battling a conversation based on how this is the most ridiculous thing he has ever heard. Good luck the next time you need a jar opened. In a nutshell, going against the grain means to do the opposite of what's expected. If you choose to go against the grain, make sure you have good reason. The pawn guarding the queen better have a meaning. There had better be a piece on the board we don't see or expect to get taken. Otherwise you're setting yourself up to lose. Many other boats by you in the water have already cut their ropes, allowing you to sink or sail. Either way, whatever happens to you won't affect them.

Having a job in Corporate is kind of like sports cars. They aren't for everyone. If you enjoy the challenges of the day-to-day battles with crabs and CEOS, let where the earth hits the ozone and the stars be your limits. If you're not built for this type of atmosphere, these laws signify that you're not crazy. Share these laws with as many people as you can to let them know where to draw the lines and limits. I wish I had read something like this to save me the hassles of going against the grain of many companies or losing many limbs to crabs I later grew back. You will grow your parts back that they kept but you will never come

48

back together the same way as you once were the day
before you entered Corporate America.

49

About Robert Greene

Robert Greene a writer and artist from Elburn, IL. He is from a family of artist and writers. Has a decorated past of many achemvents and awards ranging from work displayed at the Milwaukee Art Museum and the Chicago Museum of Contemporary Art.

His work has been featured in the Wisconsin State, Journal, Wisconsin Times and varous radio shows. It is Roberts goal to provide books that use real life situaions and solutions. He takes pride in giving his readers the tools that can help them through current and past situations.

Made in United States
Troutdale, OR
03/22/2025

29965154R00031